DEMI LOVATO

Kathleen Tracy

Mitchell Lane
PUBLISHERS

P.O. Box 196
Hockessin, Delaware 19707
Visit us on the web: www.mitchelllane.com
Comments? email us: mitchelllane@mitchelllane.com

PUBLISHERS

Printing 1 2 3 4 5 6 7 8 9

A Robbie Reader
Contemporary Biography

Abigail Breslin
Aly and AJ
Brenda Song
Dakota Fanning
Demi Lovato
Dr. Seuss
Eli Manning
Jaden Smith
Jimmie Johnson
Jordin Sparks
Miley Cyrus
Selena Gomez
Syd Hoff
Tony Hawk
Albert Pujols
Amanda Bynes
Brittany Murphy
Dale Earnhardt Jr.
Donovan McNabb
Dwayne "The Rock" Johnson
Emily Osment
Jamie Lynn Spears
Johnny Gruelle
LeBron James
Miranda Cosgrove
Shaquille O'Neal
Tiki Barber
Alex Rodriguez
Ashley Tisdale
Charles Schulz
David Archuleta
Drake Bell & Josh Peck
Dylan & Cole Sprouse
Hilary Duff
Jesse McCartney
Jonas Brothers
Mia Hamm
Raven-Symoné
Story of Harley-Davidson
Tom Brady

Library of Congress
Cataloging-in-Publication Data
Tracy, Kathleen.
Demi Lovato / by Kathleen Tracy.
p. cm. — (A Robbie reader)
Includes bibliographical references and index.
ISBN 978-1-58415-754-0 (library bound)
1. Lovato, Demi, 1992- —Juvenile literature. 2. Actors—United States—Biography—Juvenile literature. I. Title.
PN2287.L656T73 2009
791.4302'8092—dc22
[B]

2009006317

ABOUT THE AUTHOR: Kathleen Tracy has been a journalist for over twenty years. Her writing has been featured in magazines including *The Toronto Star*'s "Star Week," *A&E Biography* magazine, *KidScreen* and *TV Times*. She is also the author of numerous biographies, including *The Historic Race for the Democratic Presidential Nomination: The Clinton View* and *The Fall of the Berlin Wall, Gwen Stefani, Mariah Carey, Johnny Depp,* and *Kelly Clarkson* for Mitchell Lane Publishers.

PUBLISHER'S NOTE: The following story has been thoroughly researched and to the best of our knowledge represents a true story. While every possible effort has been made to ensure accuracy, the publisher will not assume liability for damages caused by inaccuracies in the data, and makes no warranty on the accuracy of the information contained herein. This story has not been authorized or endorsed by Demi Lovato.

PLB

TABLE OF CONTENTS

Words in **bold** type can be found in the glossary.

Music has been part of Demi Lovato's life since she was a young child, but she later discovered a love for acting as well. "Music comes more natural," she says, "but I have a true passion for acting." In her Disney Channel series, *Sonny with a Chance*, Demi is able to combine her two performing sides.

The World's Biggest Stage

Demi Lovato couldn't believe it. She was going to perform at a kids' concert to honor soldiers and their families in Washington, D.C. It was part of Barack Obama's **inauguration** (in-aw-gyuh-RAY-shun) celebration—and it would be the biggest performance of her life. "It's a huge honor and I'm ridiculously nervous," she admitted before the concert. "I don't know what I will be able to do with myself." Her biggest worry? "I really hope I don't fall!"

The performance took place the night before Obama was sworn in as president of the United States. The concert was hosted by Michelle Obama and Jill Biden, wife of Vice

President-elect Joe Biden. In the audience were **First Kids** Sasha and Malia Obama. Demi told MTV News it was fun meeting the First Family. "Michelle Obama is way down to earth. She gave me a hug, and her daughters were so sweet. You could tell they are not fazed by anything."

Malia (left), Sasha, and Michelle Obama enjoy the Kids' Inaugural Concert in 2009. Michelle Obama praised Demi and the other performers. "You kids are the future of this great nation," she said.

Demi has appeared with Miley Cyrus and the Jonas Brothers at several concerts. Despite her success, Demi admits she can still get starstruck when meeting other celebrities. "There have been times where I definitely made a fool of myself and embarrassed myself by getting too starstruck. But it has calmed down a little bit."

Also appearing with Demi were Miley Cyrus, Bow Wow, Usher, and the Jonas Brothers. All the performers were excited. Nick Jonas told MTV News, "We could not have been more thrilled."

During the concert, Demi sang "Get Back" and "La La Land." She admitted to MTV News the day after the concert that it was an

After costarring with the Jonas Brothers in *Camp Rock* and opening for them in their 2008 tour, rumors swirled that Demi and Nick Jonas were a romantic couple. Demi denies the reports. "I just think it's funny." She does acknowledge, though, "Any girl that is a friend of the Jonas Brothers gets hate mail and is automatically suspected as a girlfriend."

emotional experience. "It was just an honor that I could make them smile when their parents are fighting in another country. And looking down in the first row and seeing [Sasha and Malia Obama] there was awesome. To see them dancing, singing, clapping, was so **surreal**."

The concert was titled The Kids' Inaugural: We Are the Future. Demi wasn't shy that night about sharing her hopes for the future: "Our economic system is in a crisis right now. I definitely hope that that will change. Also, I hope that the war resolves. Whether we win or lose or whatever, it doesn't matter. I hope that it just ends. I think that Barack Obama will be able to help us."

Demi thinks it's important for kids to get involved in politics. "That was the great part about the Kids' Inaugural," she said during the MTV News interview. "I got to be involved in something that was history-making."

Nobody who knows Demi was surprised. Even as a young child in Texas, Demi was destined to make history.

Texas-born Demi was excited to sing the national anthem before the start of a Dallas Cowboys football game in November 2008. But even though her mom was once a Dallas Cowboys cheerleader, Demi admits she's not a football fan: On Super Bowl Sunday, she spent the day watching an *America's Top Model* marathon instead of the game.

Lone Star Girl

Demetria Devonne Lovato was born August 20, 1992, in Dallas, Texas. Her mother, Dianna, was a Dallas Cowboys Cheerleader in 1983. She also pursued a career as a country singer. Demi proudly told the *Washington Post*, "I got my voice from her." Performing runs in the family. Demi's sister Dallas, who is five years older, is also a singer and an actress.

Dianna divorced Demi's father, Patrick, in 1994. Afterward, he moved to New Mexico, so Demi rarely saw him as she was growing up. Dianna remarried in 1995, and Demi has become close to her stepfather, Eddie De La Garza. She says they have a close-knit family, which now includes her younger sister,

Madison. She is proud to be **multiethnic** (mul-tee-ETH-nik), with an Irish, Italian, and Hispanic **heritage** (HAYR-ih-tij).

Demi's first performance was in kindergarten. She told Laura Yao of the *Washington Post*, "I knew from the second I stepped onstage. I was like, yep, this is what I want to do."

Her first professional job was playing Angela on *Barney & Friends*. During the **audition** (aw-DIH-shun), she met her future BFF, Selena Gomez. Demi says there were 1,400 kids at the audition. "We sat next to each other in line and made friends." Both Demi and Selena were cast and appeared on the show in 2002. "And ever since then, we've just had a great friendship."

Demi enjoyed acting but loved music. She said on a 2009 press tour, "When I was around eight, my mom came to me with the idea of songwriting. So I always had it in the back of my [mind] but it never came out of me until about the seventh grade." Once she started, Demi said, she couldn't stop.

Demi comes from a close-knit family. Her mom, Dianna (left) credits family dinners. "We all like to get together in the kitchen while preparing dinner because it gives us time to talk about our day and allows us to bond as a family."

"Since then I've written probably around like 200 to 300 songs. It's kind of like **therapy** for me. It is what I do in my spare time and I can't live without it. I have my mom to thank for that."

Her musical talent would eventually make her a star. But first, Demi would suffer through some hard times.

As she gets older, Demi says, her fashion sense is changing. "I usually wear lots of black . . . but I've been dressing more 'girly' lately because I'm more confident. I even have PINK nail polish on my toes now, which is weird because I haven't worn that since like, eighth grade."

CHAPTER THREE

Darkest Before the Dawn

After *Barney*, Demi's career stalled. Audition after audition ended in disappointment. Even worse, Demi started getting bullied at school. "I went through a really hard time," she admitted to Yao. "I blamed it on myself at the time, but looking back I guess [I was bullied] out of **jealousy**."

The taunting caused Demi to lose her self-confidence. "I'd gone through so much rejection at that point with girls at school that I couldn't do acting anymore, where all I was doing was working hard and hearing *no*." Tired of the rejection, Demi decided to quit for a while. She also left the school and started homeschooling.

Quitting performing for a while turned out to be a blessing. "I started missing it," she told Yao. Demi was surprised to realize she missed acting just as much as singing. "I always thought that music was my number one

Demi and Selena Gomez have been best friends since they met on the set of *Barney & Friends*. Their careers can make it difficult to spend time together, but they keep in touch on the phone and through Twitter.

passion. But when I quit I realized that I have a true passion for acting, and that's when I picked it back up again."

Once she started auditioning again, she said, "things started rolling. I think that's because there was a new drive in it, there was more passion than there was before."

In 2006, Demi appeared in the FOX series *Prison Break* and on an episode of *Just Jordan* on Nickelodeon. Then in early 2007, she auditioned for a new Disney Channel series called *As the Bell Rings*. Demi admitted during the press tour interview that the thought of being on the Disney Channel freaked her out. "I went to my acting coach, I was crying. I said, 'I'm not funny. I just can't do it.' I never thought that I would be funny enough to be on Disney Channel."

She thought wrong. Demi was cast as Charlotte Adams. The series **premiered** on August 26, 2007. She appeared in only eight episodes, but her talent caught the attention of Disney executives. Demi was about to be offered the break of a lifetime.

Demi says the Jonas Brothers are more than just tour mates; they are three of her closest friends. They worked with Demi on her debut album, *Don't Forget*, and are featured on the single "On the Line," which they wrote with Demi. "I tend to write songs that are a little bit more intense and I needed help writing catchy songs," she says.

CHAPTER FOUR

Breakout

In early 2008, Demi was cast as Mitchie Torres in *Camp Rock*. Her costars were the Jonas Brothers. The movie premiered on June 20, 2008, and changed her life forever. Demi was suddenly a star. But she reminds everyone that this was no overnight success. "It's been about eight years in the making."

After the movie aired, Demi said, her life became a whirlwind. "It actually started to change [while I was] doing press for the movie. Right after that, I started working on my album. Right after *that*, I started touring."

She first went on a solo concert tour. When that ended, she joined the Jonas Brothers in their 2008 Burnin' Up tour. "It's definitely been extremely **intimidating** to work with people who are as known as the Jonas Brothers," she admitted. "But what I've learned is that the more people that you work with, the more you realize they are just people."

Demi, who plays guitar, piano, and drums, admitted in a Tommy2.net interview that she was nervous the first time she performed in front of a huge crowd. "I was crying and scared. Selena [Gomez] was there with me, and she was like 'You've got to pull it together.' So that was pretty funny."

The tour lasted all summer. She called it "the most crazy fun insane experience I've ever had in my life." But she denied rumors she and Nick Jonas were dating. In fact, she swears she doesn't have a crush on any of them. "I think I'm the only girl in America who doesn't," she joked to the *Washington Post*.

In September 2008, Demi released her first solo album, *Don't Forget*. It sold nearly 100,000 copies the first week. Her dream was coming true. And it was only the beginning.

Demi is determined to be an all-around performer. In addition to being a talented singer and actress, she is also a skilled musician and plays the piano, guitar, and drums. Demi says her musical tastes are expanding. "I never used to listen to anything but rock, but I've been listening to different genres of music lately," she says, including Aretha Franklin, Billie Holiday, John Mayer, Duffy, and Phantom Planet.

Between working on the Disney series, *Sonny with a Chance*, and her music career, Demi is too busy to hang out or go shopping. "I really like to shop at Urban Outfitters. If I had time to splurge, I think I would splurge more, but I don't really find time to."

CHAPTER FIVE

Demi's Chance

In 2008, Demi and Selena filmed *Princess Protection Program* for Disney Channel. Demi says in *Teen Magazine*, "Almost every scene we did, Selena would say, 'Oh my gosh—we're shooting a movie right now!' It just hit us! We met each other the day we started working on [our careers], so it's pretty ironic."

Like Selena, who stars in Disney's *Wizards of Waverly Place*, Demi now lives in Los Angeles. In late 2008, she began taping her new Disney series, *Sonny with a Chance*. In it she plays a girl from the Midwest who wins a contest to star in a popular TV series.

Despite her head-spinning success, Demi credits her parents for keeping her grounded and out of trouble. She said, "It's definitely the way that I was raised. My faith is strong, and my parents are incredible. They're there for me. I can talk to them about anything, no matter what. They're 100 percent supportive."

Because of her upbringing, Demi is comfortable being a role model. Just don't expect her to be perfect. "There's a point where you've gotta not care, otherwise you put too much pressure on yourself and then you turn crazy. The way I want to be a role model is not by not making mistakes. What makes an impact on people is when you do something [positive]."

Demi wants fans to realize success doesn't always equal fun. "People think that if you have a nice purse in your hands, your life is fabulous and that's not it," she said in a January 2009 *Teen Hollywood* interview. She knows she and other friends like Selena and Miley Cyrus have a lot to be thankful for. "But there is also a lot that people don't see; how much we work, how much we are separated from our families, being trashed online."

Demi is comfortable being a role model and regularly attends functions benefiting kids, including the 2008 Arthur Ashe Kids' Day. She also believes in being politically involved. In April 2009 she used Twitter to urge teachers and other educators to stop bullies from abusing other students in school.

Miley Cyrus (center) says rumors of a feud between her, Demi (left), and Selena Gomez were overblown. "I love Demi and she always is there for me. She is one of my bestest friends." The three Disney stars hung out at a Grammy party in February 2009. When their schedules permit, they enjoy going out for sushi.

Although many of Demi's dreams have already come true, there is still a lot she'd like to achieve. "I would love to win a Grammy one day," she says. "I'd also like to sky dive and maybe have my own cereal one day!"

In the end, though, all the sacrifices are worth it. She continues, "When we get to see the rewards that our sacrifices have given us, it's just incredible, and that's why we continue to do what we love."

And Demi Lovato plans to keep doing that for a long time to come.

CHRONOLOGY

1992 Demetria Devonne Lovato is born August 20 in Dallas, Texas.

1994 Her parents divorce.

1995 Her mother marries Eddie De La Garza.

2002 Demi, along with Selena Gomez, begins acting on *Barney & Friends*.

2006 After a dry spell in her acting, she appears on *Prison Break*.

2007 She appears on *Just Jordan*, then lands the role of Charlotte in *As the Bell Rings*.

2008 She is cast in *Camp Rock*. She goes on a solo concert tour, then joins the Jonas Brothers on their Burnin' Up tour. Her first album, *Don't Forget*, debuts at #2 on Billboard's Top 200 album chart. She performs for the City of Hope charity. She works with Selena Gomez on the movie *Princess Protection Program*. She begins working on the series *Sonny with a Chance*.

2009 She performs her music at The Kids' Inaugural: We Are the Future in Washington, D.C. Her series *Sonny with a Chance* debuts. She stars with the Jonas Brothers again in *Camp Rock 2*.

FILMOGRAPHY

2009 *Camp Rock 2* (TV movie)
Sonny with a Chance (series)
Princess Protection Program (TV movie)

2008 *Camp Rock* (TV movie)

2007 *As the Bell Rings* (series)
Just Jordan (series)

2006 *Split Ends* (series)
Prison Break (series)

2002–03 *Barney & Friends* (series)

DISCOGRAPHY

2008 *Don't Forget*
Camp Rock Soundtrack

FIND OUT MORE

Books

Johns, Michael-Anne. *Just Jonas! The Jonas Brothers Up Close and Personal.* New York: Scholastic, 2008.

Reusser, Kayleen. *Selena Gomez.* Hockessin, Delaware: Mitchell Lane Publishers, 2010.

Ryals, Lexi. *Best Friends Forever: Selena Gomez & Demi Lovato.* New York: Price Stern Sloan, 2008.

FIND OUT MORE

Works Consulted

This book is based on the author's interview with Demi Lovato during Winter Press Tour, January 16, 2009, and on the following other sources:

Barker, Lynn. "Demi Lovato Takes a 'Chance.' " *Teen Hollywood*, January 17, 2009,
http://www.teenhollywood.com/printerversion.asp?r=195087

BuddyTV, Jonas Brothers Living the Dream,
http://www.buddytv.com/articles/jonas-brothers-living-the-dream/jonas-brothers-demi-lovato-sou-25785.aspx

Coleman, Judy. "At Sweet 16, Lovato's Ready for Her Close-Up." *Boston Globe*, September 23, 2008, p. 8SID.

"Demi Lovato, Selena Gomez." *Teen Magazine*, October 2008,
http://music.spreadit.org/demi-lovato-selena-gomez-teen-magazine-cover-interview/

Rosario, Mariela. "Demi Lovato Gushes About Performing for Obamas at Kids' Inaugural Concert." Latina.com, January 21, 2009,
http://www.latina.com/entertainment/music/demi-lovato-gushes-about-performing-obamas-kids-inaugural-concert

Sonny with a Chance production material from Disney.

Ultimate Selena. *Demi Lovato Interview.* January 21, 2009,
http://ultimateselena.com/2009/01/demi-lovato-interview-excerpts-from-teen-hollywood/

Vena, Jocelyn. "Demi Lovato Says Playing For Obama Girls Was 'Surreal.'" *MTV News*, January 20, 2009,
http://www.mtv.com/news/articles/1603075/20090120/lovato__demi.jhtml

———. "Jonas Brothers, Demi Lovato Get Inauguration-Show Jitters." *MTV News*, January 16, 2009,
http://www.mtv.com/news/articles/1602952/20090116/jonas_brothers.jhtml

Yao, Laura. "Disney Demi-Goddess—'Camp Rock' Likely to Catapult Teen Into Stardom." *Washington Post*, June 21, 2008, p. C1.

On the Internet

Demi Lovato: Official Site
http://www.demilovato.com/

Sonny With a Chance: Official Site
http://tv.disney.go.com/disneychannel/sonnywithachance/index.html

GLOSSARY

audition (aw-DIH-shun)—To try out for a part in a play, movie, or other type of performance.

First Kids—The children of the president of the United States.

heritage (HAYR-ih-tidj)—The culture or ethnic group of one's ancestors and/or relatives.

inauguration (in-aw-gyuh-RAY-shun)—A ceremony at which someone is sworn into office (to officially assume a job).

intimidating (in-TIH-mih-day-ting)—To fill with awe or worry.

jealousy (JEH-luh-see)—To be angry or upset that you don't have what someone else has or achieves.

multiethnic (mul-tee-ETH-nik)—To have relatives from more than one race, country, or religion.

premiere (preh-MEER)—The first time a performance is shown.

surreal (suh-REEL)—To feel like a dream; to seem unreal.

therapy (THAYR-uh-pee)—Treatment for an illness, injury, or mental disorder.

PHOTO CREDITS: Cover, pp. 1, 3, 22—Carlos Alvarez/Getty Images; pp. 4, 8— Ethan Miller/Getty Images; p. 6—AP Photo/Department of Defense, Yeoman 1st class Donna Lou Morgan; p. 7—Lester Cohen/WireImage/Getty Images; p. 10—AP Photo/L.M. Otero; p. 13—Arnaldo Magnani/Getty Images p. 14—Jeffrey Mayer/WireImage/Getty Images; p. 16—K. Mazur/TCA 2008/WireImage/Getty Images; p. 18—Eric Charbonneau/Le Studio/WireImage; pp. 21, 25—Andrew H. Walker/Getty Images; p. 27—Kristian Dowling/Getty Images. Every effort has been made to locate all copyright holders of material used in this book. If any errors or omissions have occurred, corrections will be made in future editions of this book.

INDEX